Help!

Whose homework *IS* this?

. . . a parents' guide: why children are given homework and what to do about it.

Jan Evans

Copyright information

Copyright © 2016 Jan Evans

First Printed August 2016

All Rights Reserved. No part of this publication or the information in it may be quoted from or reproduced in any form by means such as printing, scanning, photocopying or otherwise without prior written permission of the copyright holder.

Disclaimer and Terms of Use: Effort has been made to ensure that the information in this book is accurate and complete, however, the Writer and the Publisher do not warrant the accuracy of the information, text and graphics contained within the book due to the rapidly changing nature of science, research, known and unknown facts and internet. The Writer and the Publisher do not hold any responsibility for errors, omissions or contrary interpretation of the subject matter herein. This book is presented solely for motivational and informational purposes only.

About the writer

Jan Evans qualified as a teacher in 1973 and taught in numerous primary schools in England, (class teacher, PE, Special Educational Needs, Reading Recovery) in a Learning Support Service and a Specific Learning Difficulties (Dyslexia) Unit. At the same time, she privately tutored children for over 30 years (the last 12 years on a full time, self-employed basis) working with children aged 5 -17 who found the day-to-day learning process in school a challenge.

This is her first book. Previously she has written the content for 'Think About!' (a listening programme for learners aged 7+ that was shortlisted for the BETT Awards), project managed 'The Sledmere Stories' (a series of reading books for reluctant readers), and designed 'Flexisound', a set of plastic folding mats to help with phonics.

You can follow Jan's blog at
www.changing-your-life.com/homework

Jan Evans - LLB (Hons), Certificate of Education, British Dyslexia Association Approved Teacher (Specific Learning Difficulties), Advanced Diploma Reading Recovery.

www.changing-your-life.com/homework
support@changing-your-life.com

For children and their families everywhere. . .

Acknowledgements

Thank you:

Adam, Alex, Amanda, Andrea, Andy, Angela, Ann, Anne, Barbara, Caitlin, Carissa, Carol, CCB, Clare, Clarice, Danica, Deb, Denise, Dylan, Ewan, Faye, Freya, Gav, George, Grace, Guy, Helen, Hilary, Jess, Jessica, Jo A, Jo W, June, Karen, Kate B, Kate F, Katie, Keith, Kelly, Linda, Liz, Lynn, Marita, Martin, Mike, Nina, Norman, Paul, Rachel, Rebecca, Richard, Rob, Rockaholic, Ruth B, Ruth H, Rosie, Stephen, Sue, Susie, Tracey, Tristan, Vanessa, Zoe, and many others who wish to remain nameless, for responding to my request way back in January 2014 for your views on homework.

The content of my book was shaped by everyday families sharing comments, opinions and real life experiences. Even though I may not have used all of your specific quotes, I am grateful for all the points you raised. I found that articles, newspapers and research studies took account of information such as yours.

It appears not much has changed over the years.

I'm indebted to Anne, whose expertise in EFT helped me when I felt blocked and I didn't want anyone to read it.

Thank you Linda M, Linda E, Mike, Tracey and Guy for gently persuading me to soften my approach, so my passion superseded the 'rant'.

Thank you inimitable Bayliss family: George, whose matter-of-fact problem solving is sheer genius; Jess, (illustrator and writer of children's books: www.jessiebayliss.com) for the cover; Tracey, for her patience, interest and proof-reading skills; and Adam, who is my 'go to guru' for dyslexic insights.

Thank you James and Rachel for the photo shoot.

Thank you Andy Calloway, (www.callowaygreen.co.uk) for setting up my website so I can use feedback on the book to link like-minded people in the homework debate. Who knows to where it may lead.

Finally, thank you family and friends. Your support and encouragement convinced me to 'go for it.'

So I did.

Jan Evans

Kinver 2016

Contents

Copyright information	ii
About the writer	iii
For children and their families everywhere...	v
Acknowledgements	vi
Contents	1
Introduction:	2
Why I wrote this, how it will help you and which options you may want to consider	2
Part 1: What homework is all about	**10**
Chapter 1: A brief history of homework in the UK	10
Chapter 2: Why homework is set and what it is expected to achieve	13
Chapter 3: What form it usually takes	23
In Primary Schools:	23
In Secondary Schools:	25
Chapter 4: Homework is a great idea	26
Chapter 5: No, it isn't	37
Chapter 6: Where do you stand so far?	51
Part 2: What to do about homework when it isn't going well ~ an overview of strategies	**53**
Chapter 7: Do the groundwork. Before your child arrives home with homework, you need to know this	57
Chapter 8: The 'WHAM' Questions	68
Chapter 9: Be prepared at home. Are you ready?	70
Chapter 10: Do it differently	76
Primary School ideas:	81
As for Secondary Schools, I have a few ideas . . .	83
Chapter 11: Opt out	86
Chapter 12: Have you changed your mind?	94
Books, articles and links references	i
Before you go . .	v

Introduction:

Why I wrote this, how it will help you and which options you may want to consider

Teaching has been my life, spanning nearly 40 years and more than 20 schools of all types. At the same time I have been privately tutoring children on an individual basis. I left State education in 2004 to focus on those children aged 5 to 17 who found school a challenge, or who weren't reading fluently by the age of 8 or more. Those who dropped though the Special Needs net came because they were deemed too bright to need help but still floundered in class. Some of these children were dyslexic and had had their self-esteem battered and destroyed along the way. They flocked to my door. I seemed to have a blue light on my head that said 'yes, you'll be safe here and learn loads.'

It's this last period, from 2004 onwards, when I was working with individual children, that inspired this book. Here's a typical scenario that I encountered time and time again with all ages. It was becoming a regular thing and seemed to be a source of great distress in many families.

"We'd had a great session.

Charlie (name changed) had had a lot of fun and his reading was improving fast. His mum was really pleased that he was making progress and said how he loved coming to me for lessons. Charlie was happy, and eager to get home to play out with his friends.
Then his mum said:
"Come on, we've got to go and do your homework, it's got to be in tomorrow and you've left it till the last minute as usual."
Charlie's 's face fell, his shoulders slumped and he started to whine.
"Do I have to? It's sunny and I promised my friend I'd call for him when I got back from Jan's. I'll do it after."
"You know it won't get done then, it will be teatime, and then dad will be home. It will only take 10 minutes."
"It NEVER takes only 10 minutes."
"Come on, the sooner we start, the sooner it will be done."
And off they would go, Charlie mumbling and protesting and his mum resigned to yet another battle over homework."

So the next time I heard the homework conversation, I asked the parent a few questions:
'Whose homework is this?'
'Why are you doing it if it's their homework?'
'How long is it supposed to take?'
'What is it for?'

I was so puzzled by their replies and blank looks that I started asking more people the same questions.

More puzzling replies.

It turns out that the homework is the child's homework, but unless the parent badgers the child to death to do it, and then finally has to step in to 'help', the homework doesn't get done. And if it is done, it sometimes takes hours (yes, hours) instead of the 10 or 20 minutes the teacher is expecting. It is accompanied by groans, reluctance, tears, and tantrums from the child and frustration, anger, threats, bribes and inner helplessness on the part of the parent.

As to what it is for, no one seemed to have a clear idea. The common thread was that homework needed to be done. Knowing what it was for was not clear. The school may have mentioned it in passing at a parents' evening or when the child transferred to the school, but usually schools expected the parents to support the child in doing it. Homework policies gave no option on it, just set out all the benefits and expectations and in some cases the sanctions if the homework was not completed.

When I started researching homework in a wider field, I found conflicting views on homework. There are no guidelines or rules. Homework is non-statutory. It is NOT compulsory. Homework is left to the discretion of each Head Teacher and each school's needs and situation.

Amongst the children I was seeing, the word 'homework' evoked reluctance, sadness, resentment and frustration, in parents and children alike. Parents felt under pressure to make the children do it and children seemed determined to avoid it at all costs, resulting in a constant triangular battle between child, parent and school. Never did any of them communicate their true feelings about what was done, or not done, behind closed doors, in either home or school.

A recurring problem with parents and children alike is the type and amount of homework that is set, particularly in primary schools, but in secondary schools too. No one seems to know what it is for, how long it should take or what to do about it. All I hear is that it causes family upset, tantrums, sulks, tears, frustration and a battle to get it done. Everyone seems to think homework is a necessary part of school life.

I wonder.

All I know is that my parents left school at 14, having escaped homework. Dad used to kick a can, read comics, get out across the fields on his bike or listen to the radio. Mum wanted a homework bag such as the scholarship girls had, but not the homework inside it. I had no homework in primary school. Once, our teacher gave us some and my friends and I were horrified - what was she thinking! We skipped out of school without it, we were too busy playing hopscotch or tearing around on bikes to do homework!

It wasn't until I got to secondary school that my evenings included homework, maybe an hour a night from when I was just 11. Perhaps I was lucky - it was well-planned, often learning vocabulary for the next lesson in a day or so, or finishing off something we had begun in the lesson. Feedback was almost instantaneous and the teachers kept a careful record of it being handed in on time. It never crossed my mind to not do it.

Getting towards exams (the dreaded O levels) there was more homework, but by then I was used to it. I didn't always like it and I remember doing it on the bus sometimes, or my friend and I doing it together to make sense of it. There was a slight uneasiness about that, as if it was 'cheating', but now I know that peer-to-peer work is vital for learning. It doesn't have to be done entirely on your own. Anyway, in most jobs now, isn't teamwork an essential requirement?

I was never overwhelmed by homework, and as for my parents 'helping' - well, mum was too busy looking after us all and dad worked endless hours in the factory and he had a second job after that. No pressure from them, just lots of moral support and a quiet place to work if I wanted. I was glad to do it myself - it meant *I* had done it and all the success would be mine. And if I made mistakes or didn't hand it in - well, that was down to me too. The learning was mine to do, not my parents'. I am very grateful for that. It was a very useful lesson.

When I was a teacher I tried not to give homework, unless someone particularly asked for some. Usually little girls, never boys. Then I may have suggested writing a story, or making up a page of sums, or telling them they had worked hard enough in school that day and just to go and play. Once I did a school assembly about square tomatoes and a whole egg in a sauce bottle. I didn't tell them how it was done and was astounded to find that many of the children went home and pestered their parents to find out. If there is a case for homework, it's to generate that excitement and wonder which will involve the whole family, but it has to come from the child's curiosity to learn, not from some artificially manufactured task which is reluctantly dragged home with resignation and resentment.

After hearing many tales of woe and misery where homework is concerned, I wanted to know what people thought about homework now, so I quizzed my students, their parents, friends, family, other teachers, and anyone else I could think of. I read articles that have been published in newspapers, education surveys and studies, policies taken from schools' websites, research undertaken by Institutes of Education, questionnaires sent out to my students and their families, and feedback from a wide range of people of all ages (4 years to 93 years old) and with diverse education experiences.

I researched the subject on the net to see how homework is perceived here in the UK and in some instances elsewhere in the world.

I found conflicting ideas and opinions, and not one unified answer to the question of giving out homework.

This was no help in resolving arguments and stress.

So the purpose of this book is to make you think about homework: what it is for and why it is set, and then for you to make up your own mind about it. Remember, homework is not compulsory. Each school sets its own policy on homework and then asks you to agree with it and support it.

This book is set out in two parts.

The first part is what homework is all about:
First of all there is a brief history of homework.
Next, an overview of what it is for, and what form it may take.
Then there'll be a chapter telling you why homework is a good idea, followed by a chapter that tells you why it isn't.
Then you could decide which camp you are in, or maybe change your mind about what you thought before you began reading this book.

The second part covers what to do about homework:
There are questions to ask your school about the homework policy. These are detailed and specific questions to make sure everyone is clear about it. There's a shortened version if you think that there may be too many.

Next, some tips on how to make sure your home is ready for when the homework gets there.

I've also included a chapter suggesting how homework could be transformed so it will be fun and a chapter in case you want to opt out of the homework brigade altogether.

Finally, the question to ask is 'what is best for **your** child?' Does homework fit with their values, dreams and aspirations, which may not necessarily be the same as yours? How will you as a family position yourselves around homework? Are you for it or against? Will you decide to stay with it, change it or opt out altogether?

I'd be pleased and intrigued to know what you decide. Drop me an email and join the discussion board there.

www.changing-your-life.com/homework
support@changing-your-life.com/homework

Part 1: What homework is all about

Chapter 1: A brief history of homework in the UK

1928: The first research on homework revealed worries about children living in poor housing. It blamed public exams for long hours of homework that interfered with hobbies and 'the development of natural abilities'.

1929: TES (Times Educational Supplement) headline: 'Homework is a nightly curse in thousands of homes and a cause of nerve trouble, sleeplessness and family friction'.

1935: Inspectors complained that teachers were still setting unsuitable tasks and argued that life for children under 10 should be homework free.

late 1930s: Homework in primary schools tended to be given only to those aged 10 who were in their final year. It was given to prepare children for the 11+ or for scholarships to secondary school. As soon as the exam had been taken, the homework ceased.

1947+: The school-leaving age was raised to 15 and it was thought that homework led to better exam results. 98% of grammar schools gave homework. 29% of secondary schools gave homework. This underlined the class divide.

1988: The introduction of the highly prescriptive National Curriculum led to a trend to formalise homework.

1995: A study by the NFER (National Foundation for Educational Research) found that 43% of 10 year olds were given no regular homework. This concerned David Blunkett, Education Secretary at the time, especially as he said that more than 50% of 10 year olds watched more than 3 hours of television a day.
Mr Blunkett said: 'Homework is an essential part of education. All the evidence suggests that homework makes an important contribution to the progress and achievement of children at school.'
(What evidence is this? Did he want children to stop watching television?)

1997: 64% of primary schools had a homework policy.

1998: Mr Blunkett announced guidelines for homework in primary and secondary schools, and support was provided for the introduction of homework clubs. These guidelines suggested that pupils as young as 4 should be doing around one hour per week, stretching to 30 minutes a day for pupils in Y5 and Y6. (ages 9 to 11). Pupils in secondary schools (11-16) should be doing up to 90 minutes per night, increasing to up to 2 ½ hours per night for those in GCSE years (15-16 year olds)

1999: 90% of primary schools had a homework policy (including 100% of junior schools and 75% of infant schools).

2013: Michael Gove, Education Secretary, scrapped the guidelines as part of an overarching plan to 'free up' head teachers, but there is no danger schools will be dropping homework.

Homework has remained a political and emotive issue for well over 80 years, even though now there are only guidelines.

Homework is non-statutory. It is NOT compulsory. Each school writes its own policy and sets its own parameters. Home school agreements do not legally have to be signed, especially as it would be difficult to enforce them.

Chapter 2: Why homework is set and what it is expected to achieve

When I asked the question 'What is homework for?' I was given varying replies from professionals, parents and children. Most replies were vague. Some people struggled to give a reason, just saying that it was expected, it was important and had to be done. When I pushed harder for specific reasons there wasn't even a consensus of opinion. Each school seemed to have its own idea, dependent on its own situation. Parents expected it. Children resisted it. Everyone grumbled about it, but no one challenged it. No one realised that homework is non-statutory and is not compulsory.

I scoured research papers, published articles and school websites.

I had to look really hard to identify why homework is set and what it is for. Very often the reasons are generic and not specific enough. As an example, when children come to me for help, and I ask about the problem, the parents have been told 'It's his writing.' Then I ask 'Is it the handwriting? Is it the content? Is it the spelling? Is it the ideas? Or the planning?' Unless I know the specific problem, it's difficult to tailor the teaching to remedy it. Similarly with the reasons for homework. It needs to be well-planned to serve a particular purpose otherwise there may not be a benefit at all.
This is a compilation of what I found, as there doesn't seem to be a common definitive policy:

Homework is set:

A. To prepare for future learning.
Sometimes students are asked to read or research a topic or new subject so that when it is presented in class they have some idea of what it is all about. It's risky, because not all students may complete it and then time is spent in class going over ground that many may have already covered for the sake of the few that didn't manage to do it. For example, Sandi Toksvig, the TV presenter, said she was told to read a book ready for the next lesson, which she did, and turned up ready to discuss it. The teacher then proceeded to make the class read the book aloud, chapter by chapter. One hopes this doesn't happen now.

B. To absorb, process and consolidate previous learning.
Most often this is perceived as important because the school day does not offer enough time to reflect on what has been learned, and also because if it is done at home, it is easier to see if the class lesson has been understood and retained.

C. To practice and reinforce something learned in class.
This highlights gaps if children have failed to understand the subject, and might need more help or a different teaching approach, or just more practice.

D. As an independent project.
This could be an extension of something started in class, or even something new, related to that work but something which

might have sparked an interest, and which can't be completed in school due to lack of time

E. To learn vocabulary, spellings or times tables.
Learning spellings and times tables seems to be important in Primary schools, to make sure children have a sound grasp of basic skills. Professor Hallam, of the Institute of Education, says 'Parents of Primary school children have for many years listened to their children read and helped with spellings and times tables. It can be done as a shared activity, even while travelling in the car. It's a way of parents showing an interest in their children's learning. Whether you call this homework is debatable. I don't think it should be banned.' (I might just add that I learned my times tables before I was 7 and I did it in school. We also learned phonics in school and never took home lists of words to learn. We were encouraged to read: anything and everything. When I was a child, homework was a foreign word.) Learning vocabulary for foreign languages, to be used in the next lesson, shows up in secondary schools.

F. To please parents, who think homework is the mark of a good school.
There is no doubt that schools are under pressure from parents to set homework. Schools that consider a homework-free approach are besieged by parents who demand homework be given. Sometimes this is because some schools finish at 3pm and parents feel children have too much time on their hands afterwards. Playing on X-boxes or going out with friends worries parents if they are not there to supervise.

Homework is a way of keeping them occupied. Private schools in particular are deemed to be short-changing parents if there is no homework.

G. To finish off class work, as the school day is too short.
The introduction of the National Curriculum meant that schools were expected to teach an increased range of subjects. Before that, primary schools followed a structured progression in Maths but were left to devise their own curriculum in other areas. Secondary schools focussed on exam syllabuses. The introduction of a National Curriculum, to be adhered to by ALL schools, meant that whichever school a child attended in the UK, they would be confident that there would be no gaps in their education - each school would follow a prescriptive content which was set for each year. This meant that all subjects had to be given a slot in the timetable. It was a complete change from a project-based approach that had reigned in Primary schools for a long time and reduced the time available for mastering foundation skills in reading, writing and maths.

H. To prepare for SATs (Standard Attainment Tests) and GCSEs (General Certificate of Secondary Education)
Schools are under pressure to perform well and achieve the targets set by Government. These tests followed on from the introduction of the National Curriculum. Government needed to know that schools were succeeding in their teaching and that children were progressing. Schools were all teaching the same subject matter so it became easy to test everyone to

see how children of the same age were performing. Very soon it became the norm to 'teach to the test'. Schools were rated on their pass rates, so in order to fulfil government targets, children would be taught material which would show up in a test. The joy of learning for learning itself had disappeared.

I remember the introduction of the National Curriculum, and I remember that my heart sank. As teachers, we sat around for hours after school, trying to make sense of a system that seemed to take no account of where children were in their learning, but enforcing a learning process that had been set to accommodate most children, but not the ones that fell outside the parameters of expectation. At one point I had a Special Needs group of children aged 7 that needed more play and investigation rather than structured instruction, but the constraints of the Curriculum and the imminent prospect of SATs meant that I had to comply with the lesson planning and reviews in line with the rest of the class. Needless to say, it didn't work.

I also remember a wonderful Summer Term with a pre-National Curriculum, Reception class (ages 5-6) where we spent 10 weeks following the nursery rhyme '1,2, buckle my shoe'. Each week we took a line of the rhyme and learned English, Maths, history, geography and science from it. One week we even went tracking in the nearby Scout Wood, (5,6 pick up sticks, 7,8, lay them straight) something that would be nigh impossible to do today. It was fun.

Alongside the reasons for setting homework, I discovered that homework is thought or expected to achieve the following:

1. It will improve Home and School relationships in a 3-way process.

This viewpoint was quoted by schools, especially where parents did not experience a comfortable relationship with the school, for whatever reason. Sometimes parents themselves may have had a negative experience of school when they were younger, and were reluctant to engage with teachers, trusting them to educate their child. Schools see homework as way of gaining parents' confidence and making it easier to work together.

2. It will encourage parents' participation in their child's education.

These days schools expect parents to help, to be interested in and share in the work that children do in school. Some parents still expect schools alone to educate children, leaving home to be a place for other things.

3. It will prepare children for secondary school.

The amount of homework there comes as a shock. Parents are often taken aback when their child goes to secondary school at the age of 11 and comes home with piles of work. The solution adopted is to prepare children for this by giving homework in Primary schools, thereby reducing the amount of pleasure in Primary and frightening the children into thinking Secondary school is a terrible place to be.

4. It will help children manage and organise their time more effectively.
This is a skill that develops over time, and is a result of having lots of things to do that need to be done. It is a moot point at what age this should be learned or developed, but in school, 4 years old is deemed a good age to begin.

5. To help children prioritise their time.
This is a tricky one, as most children do not have complete control over the time spent at home. Very often, their time is directed by family activities. Fitting homework in may depend on what else is going on at home, and priorities may clash.

6. To encourage and develop independent learning.
Some time ago I was reading about the Long Range Desert Group, who operated in the desert during the Second World War. Can you imagine finding your way in the desert by relying on the rudiments of astro-navigation and how to use a theodolite, and the lives of your fellow companions depending on your accuracy and skill? Mike Sadler (SAS) was trained by Lofty Carr (LRDG) to do this in a few weeks. Mike said, 'I learned navigation quickly because I was interested in it, and when you are interested in it, you learn.' For me, that sums up what independent learning is all about.

7. To prepare for life.
It would be useful to know which areas of life in particular would be benefited by homework. As it stands, this expectation is too vague to be helpful.

8. To improve grades and academic success.

Homework in secondary schools has always been used for this effect. The trend has filtered into Primary schools now, so children are graded on their progress as soon as they enter pre-school at the age of 2. By the age of 6 or 7 children are given tests in SATs, settling them into a life of grades, academic progress, tests and exams. The key word here is 'academic'. There are 8 forms of intelligence and schools focus on two. The other six are not considered important enough to develop or measure. Schools are graded by Ofsted (The Office for Educational Standards) and compete for top places in league tables. Schools are under a lot of pressure to do well. Homework is one way of encouraging pupils to attain better results.

9. To support and stretch classroom learning.

The school day now is not long enough for this to happen. The only available time is after school, at home.

10. To enhance ambition.

In some schools in deprived areas, homework is seen as a way to motivate children and increase their self-belief and ambition. The feedback from teachers builds a relationship between pupil and teacher and it has a higher value if the work has been done independently, in their own time.

11. To prepare for work.

Balancing work and family life requires self-discipline, prioritising and organisation. Homework is thought to develop these important life skills. It sounds admirable in the context of students aged 15 or over. Does it apply to 4 year olds?

12. To prepare for secondary school.
Secondary school is a different environment from that in Primary. How soon should children be prepared in advance for the transition, if at all? All new stages in life come with a learning curve. Does this mean we should pre-empt all of them and prepare for everything before it happens?

13. To develop a work ethos, a habit.
This sends a message that taking work home is a good idea. As a nation we prioritise work above all other aspects of life. When I was a young teacher, I could not take time off when my son had his tonsils out - work came first. From an early age we are telling our children that not only is it acceptable to take work home, it is mandatory. As well as working 5 days out of 7, we need to take work home too. Is this a quality that needs to be included in life today?

14. To broaden experience.
This all depends on whether you think school is the only source of learning. Experience can be broadened in many ways. Some of it may be influenced by what is being learned in school; some of it may be motivated by activities out of school. It's a fine line between which has the greater impact and which takes priority.

15. To promote higher achievement.
This appears to indicate that higher achievement depends on doing more work, rather than working smart. The more hours you put in, the greater your achievement. Is this always the case?

16. To teach study skills.
The skills could be taught in school. Perhaps learning study skills at home means putting them into practice.

17. To teach children how to make decisions.
This could be linked with time management - deciding what to do when, and how long to spend on something. It's not clear which decisions will be helped by doing homework.

18. To build character.
This could encompass such qualities as perseverance, diligence, doing one's best, taking a pride in quality work, setting goals for oneself, monitoring one's own progress and doing the right thing even when no one is watching.

19. To be responsible for their own learning and mistakes.
This is a useful life skill. Again, at what age is it a good idea to introduce this and is homework the only way of doing it?

Chapter 3: What form it usually takes

In Primary Schools:

1. It may be self-contained, often consisting of repetitive paper and pen exercises, filling in words, related to English, history, geography, science or topic. Parents are quite keen on this because it's easy for them to monitor and understand. Children resist it because it's boring.
2. Pages of Maths to practice what has been learned in class.
3. Something that is too easy or something that is too hard. This is often the result of a generic piece of homework that is expected to suit everyone and be easier to set and to mark.
4. A project, lasting perhaps half a term, where your child has to do some research and put information together in some detail. It may be an extension of the school topic current at the moment e.g. "Research the party leaders who are standing in the General Election. Which one would you choose for Prime Minister and why." (This example was actually given to a 9 year old). It might involve computers, research or completing a Maths assignment on the Internet and might need some adult assistance or guidance.
5. Spellings. Learning a list of words that may be linked to phonics being learned in class. They may be words linked to the current topic in history, science or geography. There may be lists of words that are commonly mis-spelt. Sometimes the

lists are for everyone; sometimes a child has a list of their own, depending on what stage they are at.

6. Making something, eg a castle - this is where dad comes into his own and proudly oversees the building, making sure it would win an award in a national contest. No shoebox designs here!

7. Preparing for a writing task later in the week. Brainstorm ideas with your parent and pre-plan it, ready to write.

8. Computer-based work.

9. Reading 'the book'. For 5-7 year olds this may be a reading book in a reading scheme, and it may be that a parent is expected to hear their child read one or two pages, or even a whole book. For 7+, if they are no longer reading the reading scheme books, children are expected to read a book they have chosen from school. These are often fiction. Non-fiction books tend to be more difficult to read, due to the advanced language that many reference books use.

10. Homework time is increased gradually: 30 mins per night in Y3 (ages 7-8) up to 18-24 hours per week for 6th formers. (16-18)

11. Learning multiplication tables up to 12 x 12.

In Secondary Schools

This comprises all sorts of things that you as a parent are bewildered by and can't do any more, even if you did get a degree in the subject.

There may be essays to write, Maths problems to solve or a project to complete. The nature of the task and how long it requires may vary, depending on the subject. For example, pupils may need to spend two hours at the beginning of a half-term designing and drawing an artifact while its construction has to take place for the rest of that half-term in school, whereas Maths and foreign languages need regular practice and execution.
Often, in later years, work is geared to exam preparation - answering exam questions in a specified time, which are then reviewed in class the next week or the next lesson.

In any event, a large bag is required to cart all the work to and from school. It can be quite a weight, and if constantly carried over one shoulder or in one hand can put a strain on pupils' backs and shoulders, due to the uneven weight distribution. It's a health hazard.

Chapter 4: Homework is a *great* idea

'She came to my door one spring day. She wanted private lessons after school for her twin daughters and an older boy. "I want you to give them lots of lovely homework as well," she said. "Lots of lovely homework." '

You found out in Chapter 2 why homework is set and what it's expected to achieve.
Let's look at this in more detail, as there are strong, persuasive reasons for children to be given homework.

There was an overlap between information from research studies, what people told me face-to-face and what I found from schools themselves. There were also differences, depending on different circumstances that schools found themselves in and what they felt their priorities to be. Remember, there are no official rules and regulations around homework; each school can decide for themselves what they want it to be, how often it is given and what form it will take. It is expected that all parents will support the school in this, and some schools ask for signatures on a contract with both parents and children agreeing to this arrangement.

I was surprised to find that parents *expect* homework to be given. Margaret Morrissey, of 'Parents Outloud' and the National Confederation for Parent Teacher Associations, says that parents feel it's the mark of a good school. John Fairhurst, head of Shenfield School in Essex puts it: "Homework is part of the traditional parents' mindset about what makes a good school." I've spoken to Head Teachers who have had parents say they will take their child away from the school if homework isn't set. Richard, one of my respondents, says in the independent schools he worked in, parents felt they were not getting their money's worth unless homework was set.

Parents want the very best for their child, especially if they themselves did not get the most out of school, for whatever reasons. Anything that will help their child reach their full potential is encouraged and some parents see homework as a way of achieving this.

Parents are also quite keen to know what their child is learning, and, if necessary, to help them with it, especially if their child is struggling in school. Peter Stanford, from The Independent, says parents don't want their child to be singled out or be seen as failing, and expect homework.
Some parents see homework as a trade-off for all the nice things they do with their children. The expectation is that 'we do nice things for you, so you need to work hard and do your homework.'

Robert Trawford, Head Teacher of a primary school in Walsall, sees homework as a key way to involve parents in their children's education. He believes it was one of the main reasons for his school's rapid improvement. (2009). He said: "Most parents now come to parents' evenings. That didn't used to be the case. Children have home-link books that say 'your child has been asked to discuss this.' I have never had a parent say they didn't want homework." The school fosters parental involvement from the moment children enter nursery, when 'Curiosity the Cat' asks them what happened on the way to school, what they saw and what they talked about with their parents. "When I came to this school I saw a parent pick up their child and carry him home without saying a word. That wouldn't have happened in my previous school," says Mr Trawford.

This home-school link remains important in building trust and home-school link books are useful in making the learning a 3-way process. Without it, some parents may never interact with the school, leaving all the teaching to teachers. Some parents think this form of education is the school's responsibility, but teachers feel differently.

In the early years (ages 5 up to about 11), teachers and parents think it's important that they hear children read and help children learn their times tables and spellings. They feel that the school day is not long enough to fit everything in, and it helps everyone to do some support work with the fundamental skills.

In addition to this, in junior school (ages 7-11, Key Stage 2) most parents expect 2 or 3 pieces of homework per week - English, Maths and some topic or project work. The reasoning behind this varies, and some of the thinking applies to all homework, whether in primary or secondary school, for all ages.

One of the main reasons put forward is that homework prepares children for secondary school. When they transfer at the age of 11, the transition is so upsetting and different that children need to be prepared for it whilst in Primary. It's a shock, especially being faced with lots of homework in addition to getting used to many teachers for many subjects, instead of one familiar teacher for everything. I've spoken to Heads, teachers and parents who have said this. "It wouldn't be fair to let them go unprepared. It's so different, and such a shock. Homework prepares them to be organised learners."

For all ages, homework is meant to help children practise and reinforce what they have learned in class. It will help them absorb and process information. They need time to do this, which isn't possible in the school day now as there's far too much to cover.

This in turn, will develop time-management and organisation. Time has to be found to complete homework as well as enjoying after school activities, and children need to learn to structure their free time to fit it all in. In doing so, children will also develop self-discipline. Parents will encourage their children to do the homework straight away. When it's done, they will have so much time afterwards to do what they want. If they leave it, the homework becomes bigger in some way, and it's a useful lesson to learn, that doing these tasks first somehow keeps them in check. An important life strategy.

There's also a potential benefit that homework will encourage independent learning and build a relationship with the teacher. Sir Robin Bosher, a former primary Head and former Primary Director for the Harris Federation of Academies, says that homework is a good thing. "When you achieve something independently in your own time, the feedback you get from the teacher has a higher value. The acknowledgement from the teacher can raise your self-esteem."

Some teachers I spoke to felt homework is important. It gives children a chance to practice and reinforce something, especially if they secretly like work but are fighting the 'working's not cool' attitude. Many pupils will not reveal in front of their peers that they do not understand something - homework may reveal these misunderstandings and let the teacher know that pupils need more help, and it can be given in a discreet manner. If many pupils don't get it, the teacher may have to re-teach it in a different way.

Some teachers see homework as a reflection of how well they are performing themselves.
If a pupil \ child gets the homework wrong or struggles with it, then the teacher can present the learning in a different way. It enhances their effectiveness as a teacher.

Homework is also a way of broadening experience, preparing for future learning and work. It can support and stretch school learning and promote research skills.

Mr Trawford says it's about being creative rather than repetitive pen and paper exercises that parents love but to which children do not respond. For example, 11 year olds in his school may do a little project of 2 or 3 pages with an illustration. He says "Homework shouldn't be some awful repetitive task. It can be linked with going to the library. If you are doing Henry VIII, you might suggest they go home and pretend Mum is Anne Boleyn and ask her questions."

Lesley Smith of Ark Schools, which runs nine primary academies, three of which are all-through schools, says homework can be made really interesting, using games and competitions, and children will then be very enthusiastic about it. If pupils don't think they are getting anything out of it, it is no use.

Independent schools firmly believe that homework is a powerful tool in the quest for academic success and preparing pupils for work. Girls in Jill Berry's school in Bedford do homework from the age of 7. As long as it's appropriate and meaningful, she believes that independent reading, and absorbing and processing what they have learned not only secures better exam results but develops self-discipline, prioritising and organisation. These qualities will be needed when decisions have to be made in balancing work and family life in the future.

Homework can become a habit, which is a good one to develop. Working extra time in anything can lead to better achievements, and it also gives pupils an edge in this competitive world we live in.

There is a belief that homework is far better than passive entertainments after school, such as watching television or playing games on computers or Xboxes. David Blunkett was very concerned that in 1995, 50% of 10 year olds watched more than 3 hours of television a day. Those figures may even have increased since then.

Time allocated by teachers for homework may start in infant school (ages 4-7) with a few pages of reading, some spellings to learn and maybe learning times tables. There's a '10 minute guideline' that is loosely applied in many schools:

All these times are for *every day*:

Y1	ages 5-6	10 mins
Y2	ages 6-7	10-20 mins
Y3\4	ages 7-9	30-40 mins
Y5\6	ages 9-11	30 mins -1hour
Y7\8	ages 11-13	1-1 ½ hours
Y9\10	ages 13-15	1 ½ hours
Y11	ages 15-16	1 ½-3 hours

It doesn't sound much, does it?

The evidence for homework leading to better results is mixed, being stronger for secondary pupils than for primary.

In 2001, Caroline Sharp's study for Ofsted (Office for Standards in Education) researched the previous 12 years in the UK and the United States. She found a link between secondary school pupils' achievement and homework for those who did a reasonable amount, but underachievers included those who did a lot and those who did a little.
A government-funded 'Effective Pre-School, Primary and Secondary Education' project showed a marked difference in attainment between 14 year olds doing 2-3 hours homework and similar pupils doing none. The pupils who did homework were found to be nearly one National Curriculum level higher in Maths, ¾ of a level higher in science and more than ½ a level higher in English at Key Stage 3.

The Guardian's education editor says 'Two hours' homework a night is linked to better school results." (29th March 2012)

Harris Cooper's work in the USA concluded that the homework link in young children could improve scores in tests involving simple mathematical skills.

Lesley Smith says homework is a vital tool for schools working in underprivileged areas. They have to do more to catch-up. Well-planned, purposeful homework helps embed what children have learned in lessons. Alongside excellent teaching and well-planned lessons, standards can be raised.

Sir Robin Bosher says homework plays a role in raising ambitions of pupils in areas of high deprivation. He says "it's about feedback, which can motivate and develop positive beliefs about achievement and can raise expectations."
It works even better if the homework is marked. The sort of marking is crucial. Dr Bethan Marshall, of King's College, London, says: "It's not worth marking pupils' work if you don't do anything with the marks."

Feedback through constructive comments and discussion is far more valuable than a specific grade or a mark out of 10. Professors Paul Black and Dylan Wiliam found that if teachers give back work with a grade and a comment, pupils only remember the grade. Their work improves if teachers make suggestions and pupils get the chance to change what they have done. Specific feedback is the most effective teaching strategy, especially if linked to praise. It looks at where a pupil is now and where they need to get to. It lets them know what they need to do to improve.

The answer to a positive homework experience may lie in the Independent sector, where homework is completed as 'prep' during an extended school day. "By having everyone complete their homework in the same circumstances, you are putting everyone on a level pegging," says Marcus Peel, Head of Malsis Prep School in Yorkshire. This view was supported by the French President Francois Hollande in October 2013, when he declared that "Independent learning should take place at the end of a school day on school premises. Such a move would even out social inequalities."

This model is quietly filtering through to the State sector, sometimes in the form of homework clubs after school. Ofsted requires good quality feedback, so homework clubs seem to be a good way to ensure that happens quickly. Professor Dylan Wiliam suggests that homework is a waste of time unless it's completed in guided hours. Public\private schools have 5 hours of school, then supervised prep. This is the best way - prep done in class with a teacher there. Otherwise a lot of time can be wasted by teachers either marking homework that is badly targeted or chasing pupils who haven't done it. The time would be better spent preparing lessons and good quality study guides.

Another way to overcome the disadvantage pupils face if their parents are less able to help and there is no quiet, appropriate place to study at home is to invite parents to stay a while longer after dropping their children off in the mornings. At Harris Primaries, this happens twice a week. Parents are invited to sit and read with their children, and teachers offer advice on how to help their children with their progress. The school also operates workshops during the last 30 minutes of the school day. Teachers explain to parents how concepts such as multiplication or long division are taught. Working parents are offered sessions at more convenient times once a term. Booklets giving advice on how to support children with homework are sent home. Homework clubs where children have access to staff and IT facilities are also on offer.

Does any of this resonate with your thoughts on homework?

Chapter 5: No, it isn't

Wow!

All those advantages for doing homework. All those expectations.

After 5 days in school and homework at least 3 times a week, children should be all set to take the world by storm. Well, the only storm I came across with the families I work with was the turmoil in the home to get homework done at all.

Cooper's study (1989a) found that with homework good schools do even better, bad schools use homework to make up for poor learning environments, poor teachers use it to compensate for lack of teaching skills and good teachers use it to achieve ambitious goals.
Homework needs to be well-planned, purposeful and meaningful. Much of the homework today is given because it's expected, not because it is necessary.

MacBeath's and Turner's study in 1990 said the 4 most common types of homework were:
1. finishing off class work and consolidation
2. self-contained homework (in Primary Schools this is often pen and paper exercises, which children dislike and parents love.)
3. project-related work
4. preparation in advance of a lesson.

Professor Hallam of the Institute of Education (2009) says that the most commonly used - consolidation - is the least effective. Future learning works best though the effects are still small.

Professor Dylan Wiliam, of the same Institute, says that homework does not make much of a difference, mainly because most of it is not well-planned.
Follow-up homework is a waste of time unless supervised.

If class work needs finishing off, does that suggest that the school day is not long enough?

Perhaps the curriculum could be trimmed and teaching quality improved.

An NFER (National Foundation for Educational Research) research study in 2009 found that Y7 (ages 11-12) wanted work that is energetic and fun and to which they could relate. Y8 (ages 12-13) wanted less writing.
"The heavy marking required of teachers could easily be reduced by cutting down on testing and setting less homework."

Younger children were more likely to do homework if it didn't involve sitting down some more after a long day at school, spent yes, you've guessed it, sitting down. If it was fun, they were more inclined to give it some time, as it didn't appear to be work and they were learning at the same time without realising it.

One of my pupils said it was more fun if mum and dad did it too, but doesn't that defeat the purpose? Indeed, project-related work is often done together, with the parent perhaps overdoing the 'help'.

A study in 2014 found that much of the homework given *is* being done by parents and not by children. Several adults have explained this to me and there are several reasons. See if this is familiar:

-'I feel a bad parent if I don't help, especially when my child doesn't understand something or gets it wrong.'
-'When the class teacher said I should do more with my child at home, I felt a bad mum. In fact, I was already doing so much, it was overloading my child. The fact was, he couldn't do it, no matter how much time I spent with him. He was tired and had had enough. I felt the teacher was making it my fault that he wasn't learning.'
-'It would never get done if I didn't help. It's hard enough to get them to admit they have any, never mind get it out of their bag and sit down and do it.'
-'I do question homework set for my younger children as it is always a battle to get them to do it. I often have to help them and just feel like I nag them instead of enjoying evenings with them.'

-'I don't want my child to fall behind. He won't get good grades, or good exam results, and then he won't get to go to University and get a good job. It's dog-eat-dog out there you know.' (I have had that exact phrase - 'dog-eat-dog' - said to me several times. Are you worried yet?)

Peter Stanford from The Independent says "Teachers set homework in the belief that it pleases parents. Parents don't disabuse them of this, even when it is exhausting their child, because they don't want him or her to be singled out or seen as failing.'

Whose homework is it? If the teacher thinks the child can do it, then they'll give something harder next time. What happens further down the line, say at University, when the parent is not there and deadlines have to be met? Surely it would be better to let the young person do the work alone in the first place and suffer the consequences if it isn't completed?

Margaret Morrissey also thinks that parental help is a problem: 'parents who see their child struggling are going to want to help them with the right answer.' This was something that bothered Head Teacher Marcus Peel. So much for independence and all those other desirable adult qualities homework is supposed to foster and develop.

Another area for concern is the time homework takes. The time allocated by schools for each year seems to be graded fairly, starting from 10 minutes a day at the age of 5 up to more than 2 hours per night for those taking GCSEs at the age of 16.

One secondary teacher said this: " No piece of homework I ever set took more than 20 minutes - think how long it took me to think of something to set and then mark 30 of them! But then that's what we're paid for.'

Maybe. That's the troubling part. Twenty minutes in school can translate to hours (yes, hours) at home. Once the child is out of the school environment and gets home, that is their free time. Who wants to take work home with them? When parents complain that homework takes forever to get done, I ask them how long it is supposed to take. Most of the time they have no idea. They just think it has to be done until it's complete, however long it takes, and it has to be done correctly. I always suggest they find out how long it should take and then allocate that amount of time to it, even when it's not finished or it's incorrect. And to let the child do it on his own. Parents can always add a note on the bottom of the homework to explain this.

On another slant, homework is often given for a 'one size fits all' and can be too easy for some and too hard for others. There's not much point in giving it if someone can't do it at all and it's way above their heads. Conversely it's a waste of time if it's too easy. It's too much to expect that each piece of homework is targeted directly at each child's level of progress. In 2009, the ATL (Association of Teachers and Lecturers) called for an outright ban on primary school homework, and strict limits on secondary school homework, saying that it was 'counter-productive'. 'It is a waste of children's and teachers' time which could be spent much more profitably on effective learning in and out of the classroom'.

Then, when homework is returned, marking becomes an issue. Often it is handed in and never referred to ever again. Sometimes it is handed back with a mark or a comment on it, but there's no follow up. Or children mark each other's homework to save time. Or there's no point marking it because 'Some parents help, which makes marking a waste of time.'

'There's no point to it. I hand it in on a Monday and it won't be marked until the end of the term. What's the point?' (shrug)

"We mark our Maths and English homework ourselves, and do it again if we get it wrong.'

If it isn't done, children are expected to stay in and do it, often in a lunchtime break. One school webpage I visited had a homework policy that stated children would lose privileges if homework was not done. A punishment then, in both cases. So much for inspiring a joy for independent learning.

Coupled with that, home-life can be noisy, distracting and unsettling. Although Sir Robin Bosher thinks homework is a good thing, he is anxious that pupils are not unfairly disadvantaged if their parents are less able to help with homework or if pupils do not have a quiet, appropriate place to study. He also points out that overloading children with homework and other activities is something to avoid. "I don't think it's useful for a child to go from one class to another, to homework, to piano practice, like a hamster in a wheel," he said.

In 2013 the French President Francois Hollande highlighted one of the main concerns - homework ingrains social inequalities between pupils: clever, motivated children in higher sets or at better schools tend to be given more homework, while less able, less motivated pupils are given less. The result is a further widening in the attainment gap. More advantaged children are also more likely to have a quiet place to study at home, with internet access, again giving them the chance to pull ahead.

In fact, a Dutch study of who benefits from homework assignments found that it only improves the achievement level of pupils from advantaged family backgrounds. Good schools do even better. Bad schools give homework to make up for a poor learning environment. Poor teachers use it to compensate for lack of teaching skills, and good teachers use it to achieve ambitious goals.

As for improving grades, the results are debatable. Professor Hallam concludes that at secondary level there was a "positive but low correlation" between doing homework and improved attainment. She also said "More homework doesn't mean better. There comes a point where it no longer has a benefit." It's also difficult to separate the effect of homework on attainment from other factors, such as home and family background.

Here in the UK, poverty blights the lives of millions of children. In the UK, 3.5 million children live in poverty. Learning is affected when children are hungry and are coping with stresses and strains of poor housing and a lack of spending money. No one learns anything when stressed.

A Children's Commission on Poverty found that parents and children are struggling to cope with our supposedly free education system. The Commission found that seven out of ten parents struggled with the cost of school, and over half said that they had to cut back on clothing, food or heating to afford these costs. School uniforms, school meals, materials and trips were the main problem costs. In February 2015 teachers in Portsmouth reported that they are helping to combat pupils' poverty out of their own money. Government funding is so little. Some primary teachers spend £100 per term on non-curriculum related materials for students: fruit for breaks, shirts and underwear for those who wear the same clothes Monday to Friday. In secondary school, teachers fund a breakfast club for all pupils from their own wages. They pay £6-£20 per month, as well as bringing in milk and cereal. The effect is astonishing: the children are more productive and less disruptive, the bullying has decreased and the children turn up on time. For families like these, equipment necessary for homework is just an extra burden on a tight budget.

Years ago, in the 1930s, children aged 10 who had homework to prepare them for the 11+, (an exam to see which secondary school the would go to when they were 11) did their homework in the only warm place in the house - the kitchen, by the fire. The rest of the house would be freezing. Nowadays, students don't choose creative subjects because they can't afford materials, therefore homework equipment - PCs, tablets, writing materials, a place to study, food, and heat places an added burden on disadvantaged families.

Harris Cooper, Professor of social psychology at Duke University in Durham, North Carolina, conducted reviews of homework research in the USA. He found that 'the homework achievement link on broader measures of achievement (unlike tests in simple mathematical skills) appears to be weak.'

Dr Penelope Weston, formerly a researcher at the National Foundation for Educational research (NFER), produced a report for Ofsted that pointed out it was difficult to identify a clear homework corollary.

Caroline Sharp's study in 2001 for Ofsted looked at research for the previous 12 years in the UK and the United States. She said: "At primary level there is no conclusive evidence that homework boosts achievement."

In 2008, Richard Rowe, Head of a Surrey junior school, said: 'If children of primary age are taught well and do a good day's work, there should be no need for homework. They should be allowed to have a childhood.'

In 2009, he decided to abolish homework. He sent a letter to parents, explaining that pupils would be encouraged to read and to do the occasional project but the school would no longer prescribe the (up to) 30 minutes a day the government recommended for children aged between 7 and 11. A Head Teacher for 18 years, he says: 'We don't think doing lots of school work in the evenings is appropriate for children of this age. You can make arguments for parents being involved, but in so many homes it causes distress and anger.'

Ofsted graded the school outstanding and Mr Rowe says he has noticed no difference in attainment since homework stopped. He wishes he had made the decision years ago, but baulked at the controversy it might cause. One parent said they didn't want their child to have any homework. Another said they wanted more, and another that it was about right. In the end it was a management decision, but parents have been supportive.

Denmark piloted 'homework-free' schools. It led to a reported fall in dropout rates and a rise in overall grades.

Tiffin School in Kingston Surrey found that homework put children off learning, so they scrapped it.

A Cape Town school in South Africa is leading the way in the education sector by doing away with homework; six months later they're seeing surprising results.

French President Francois Hollande declared an end to homework in primary schools. "Work should be done at school rather than at home," he pronounced.

What homework does produce is stress. As far back as 1929, the TES (Times Educational Supplement) complained that 'Homework is the nightly curse in thousands of homes and a cause of nerve trouble, sleeplessness and family friction.'

Professor Hallam (Institute of Education) suggested that the damage to the relationship between parents and children, as middle class parents put pressure on their offspring to succeed, outweighed any educational advantage. She stated that 'Homework can create anxiety, boredom, fatigue and emotional exhaustion in children who resent the encroachment on their free time'. This has come about due to schools being worried about SATs (Standard Attainment Tests), so they set lots of written work to be done at home. Parents have stressful jobs and limited time, so they want quality time with their children, not having to help them with their homework.'

Margaret Morrissey, director of Parents Outloud, says: 'Schools need to explain to parents that they want their pupils to be fresh and excited in class. Younger children go to school quite early and, if their parents work, don't get home till 6pm. To have homework on top of that just risks burnout.'

'It's too much. I work till 5.30pm, get home, it's tea then bed. There's no downtime.'
Where does homework fit in there?

Some children leave homework till the last minute and then there's a battle of wills. No learning is achieved in this stressful situation and it damages the parent \ child relationship. It encroaches on time that could be spent on other, more pleasurable activities, such as seeing friends, doing things as a family, out of school activities where learning is taking place, being a child or just learning to be bored. Boredom is a breeding ground for creativity, which is a major component of successful entrepreneurship. You could easily imagine to what it might lead.

Mental health in primary school children is already an issue. There is pressure from parents, the school and the government to succeed and achieve. Schools expose children to 'booster classes' to improve their SATs results, ostensibly to help children get a higher grade 'because they're capable of it and it helps them reach their potential' but in reality it is to satisfy government targets. In some schools, Y6 children (aged 10-11) are doing yoga to relax them from the stress of SATs.

A recent headline in the Manchester Evening News proclaimed that 'Children as young as 10 worry about performing poorly in their SATs and how it could affect their future.'

More than half of children surveyed said they were anxious about not achieving Level 4 (the National Standard) in Maths, Science and English. A quarter of parents said their child was too nervous to eat before SATs exams, with 14 per cent saying they had refused food.'

It sends the wrong message about a work \ life balance. From the age of 4 we are telling children they HAVE to take work home.

'I've worked hard all day at school and I'm tired when I get home.'

'I'd rather be in the garden, playing football or watching TV.'

'It's useless, it is given to us to invade our free time at home.'

In 1928 research blamed public exams for long hours of homework that interfered with hobbies and "the development of natural abilities."

Children resent the encroachment on their free time and Margaret Morrissey has called the setting of holiday projects an "unforgivable" imposition on free time. Homework dictates how we should spend time with our children and as a family. It reduces the spontaneity and the time available for children to pursue those interests that they want to discover and learn for themselves. A follow up in 2011 to a UNICEF Childhood Report stated loud and clear that children said they would like more family time and the opportunity to play out.

Perhaps it's time to give children their childhood back, get rid of homework for good, find out what children are good at and develop that.

Chapter 6: Where do you stand so far?

Now you have an idea of the history of homework, why it is set, what form it can take and some statistics and opinions as to whether it is a good thing or not.

The next part of the book gives you practical strategies to deal with homework.

There are pertinent questions to ask of school that will make it clear for you, your child and school how homework is presented and marked.

There are tips on how to handle homework when it arrives in your home.

There are suggestions on how to do homework differently or even opt-out of it altogether.

The choice is yours. All the information will be invaluable in helping you decide where you stand in the homework debate, and the questions you raise will alert schools that you are thinking about it.

Perhaps while you are reading the strategies, keep this in the back of your mind:

Ask yourself what you really want for you and your family. Discuss with your child (even 5 year olds have an opinion) and see how they feel about it. Talk about what school was like for you. Are you replicating that through your children or doing it differently?

Search your heart and conscience. Reflect on the following (there are no right or wrong answers, just something to consider):

What qualities would you like your child to develop?

Does this match with school expectations?

Does homework reflect these values, and enhance them?

Are you prepared to stand back and let your child learn by their mistakes?

Are you prepared to let your child take the consequences if they do not do their homework?

How important to you is the quality of your family life and how you spend the time together?

Then read the chapters on what questions to ask and how to handle homework when it gets to your house.

Doing homework differently may appeal to you.

Opting-out altogether could make you furious or decide to do it.

You can still have excellent standards but the happiness and well-being of you and your family has to trump everything, and that comes from within.

You can choose.

Part 2: What to do about homework when it isn't going well ~ an overview of strategies

Schools set homework and although it is non-statutory (not compulsory) schools will encourage it for a variety of reasons:

    1. Parents expect it.

    2. There are so many subjects to cover in the National Curriculum, homework is a way of managing them all.

    3. Schools are driven by government targets, SATs results and league tables. Headteachers are pulled between doing what is best for each child and conforming to government directives. The two things are not always compatible.

From my research and observations it's clear that many parents are keen on homework.
You may be one of them and be perfectly happy with homework. Your child may love it. You may be prepared to devote your time and resources to support the school and your child in working out of school hours. You may feel that homework is part and parcel of life today and is necessary to train your child in the way the world works for you.
Perhaps you expect homework to be given right from when children enter pre-school. You want the best for your child and want to be involved in your child's education.
You are interested in what your child does in school. You don't want them to struggle and will happily help with anything that will make it easy for your child to do well. Some parents will even buy books for their child to practice handwriting, Maths

and English. Perhaps read the questions about doing the groundwork in Chapters 7, 8, and 9 and you may find that homework becomes a pleasure and much, much easier.

On the other hand, you may not be perfectly happy with homework. You might be one of those families where homework impacts on your home life in many negative ways and you are not sure what to do about it. In the beginning, homework seemed harmless - read this book with your child, practice these sounds, draw a picture . . . . These tasks may only take a few minutes, they fit into a short slot after tea or before bedtime and it is easy to persuade a child to complete them.
But as the child progresses through school, the tasks get longer and more difficult. In some households homework runs along easily, with compliant children working hard and finding homework easy to fit in and not a chore. In other homes there are problems: children resist doing it, there are arguments and upsets about completing it, it takes over weekends and family time, and often parents will spend hours helping their child to do it, or even end up doing it for them.
If this sounds like your family, read the groundwork questions in Chapters 7 and 8. Read Chapter 9 and be prepared for when homework arrives. See what a difference it makes.

Maybe this next scenario could be you. Even though you feel under pressure to be a 'good' parent, and your home life is under siege, you may want to carry on as you are. It is scary to step out of line and do something different. You may not feel like rocking the boat - yet. But it might only be a matter of time before something needs to change. Keep this book on one side for when that happens. Follow the steps in Chapters 7, 8, and 9. Maybe try something different and transform it or even opt out altogether. There is always a choice.

What follows is an overview of some strategies to help manage the problems, with more detail in the relevant chapters:

1. Make sure your child is clear on what the tasks are, how long they should take, and what to do if they don't know or are not sure.
2. Find out from the school what your role is to be concerning homework - are you expected to help?
3. Make sure there is a space at home dedicated to doing homework, complete with all the tools required.
4. If there is any problem at all, please talk to the teachers to let them know. Very often teachers are not aware of problems because parents battle on to get the homework completed. You don't have to struggle on your own. Try sending a note to discuss the issue face-to-face, or a phone call, or a 5-minute exchange before or after school. Try to get it resolved immediately. Leaving it for parents' evening will mean a hurried conversation (you know you only get about 10 minutes to discuss everything) and the problem may have got bigger in the meantime.
5. If these strategies are not effective, then it may be time to take action of a different sort. For example: talking to other

parents, making a case for reducing the workload, doing it differently or even not doing homework at all.

There are always options and choices. Read on for help in deciding what you think is best for your child and how to achieve it.

Chapter 7: Do the groundwork. Before your child arrives home with homework, you need to know this

If you have decided that homework is indeed a good thing, then make sure that everyone (parent, child, teacher) knows the parameters. Set up an appointment specifically for this purpose. The time slot you are given for parents' evenings is too short for a discussion of this sort. If homework is important, it deserves more than 10 minutes to talk about it.

You might want to ask the school the following questions about their homework policy.
There are a lot, but read them through. Chapter 8 provides a simple way of condensing them so when you ask in school, no-one feels overloaded or it's some sort of grilling.
If you like, go straight to Chapter 8 (the 'WHAM' questions) for an overview and then come back to read more detail here.

A good time to have this discussion is when your child transfers from infants to juniors, junior to secondary or even from class to class. Make a point of asking each teacher at the beginning of the school year in September what the homework policy is - it may have changed in the holiday and each year may mean more time being spent on homework and each teacher may have their own interpretation of it. It might even depend on the subject. Art, for example, requires more time than Maths.

If you know what the parameters are, then you can support the school in what is expected from your child.
Communication is vital. Work together with school from the start to prevent problems getting bigger.

Many of the parents I spoke to felt they were bad parents or failures if their child did not do their homework, did not complete it, did not understand it, or couldn't do it. They felt honour-bound to 'help' so their child would not look stupid and they would not feel they were bad parents. Just tell the teacher what is going on. Your child's troubles may be as a result of unclear communication or misunderstanding and could easily be remedied.

1. What sort of homework is given, and what is it for? (see Chapter 2 for reminders)

It might be to develop research skills, or to help with future lessons if set beforehand.

After a lesson there is an opportunity for reinforcement. It might be to help your child be responsible in meeting deadlines, to develop self-discipline. Are they ready for this and is it something you are happy for them to learn? You may want your child to have a childhood free from such things until they reach secondary school.

2. How often is it given?

There are often set days for handing it out and giving it in. There may be a gap of a few days between the two, giving your child a chance to fit it in with their busy after-school life.

There may be a danger they will leave it till the last minute but this is part of the learning process in managing their time and responsibilities.

3. How long should homework take?

Some parents of the children I work with are under the impression that they have to toil away until it is done, often taking several hours (yes, hours) and everyone is frazzled, argumentative and upset.

Find out how long it should take. Set a timer for your child to see and when the timer goes off, stop. Write a note to the teacher to say what has been achieved in the time allotted and leave it at that.

If your child wants to complete it, and is desperate to do so, let them, but add a note to say how much extra time has been spent on it. If the teacher knows this, they will have a much better idea of how long the homework is actually taking and this will mean the next lot will be set accordingly. If you don't tell them, they won't know.

In my experience, teachers set 20 minutes but the reality is it often takes an hour or more. Talk to each other!

4. When should homework be handed in?

What are the penalties or sanctions if the homework is late \ is not done at all \ is incomplete?

Find out before you start, so you and your child are clear about repercussions if homework is not done. Both of you decide if this is fair. If not, have a discussion with school to come to some agreement that everyone finds satisfactory. Remember, it's your free time that is on the line here.

5. Suppose the homework is handed in late or not at all?

It is part of your child's training in self-discipline to remember to hand it in. Not yours. DO NOT rush into school, making yourself late, to hand in homework if it has been forgotten. Let your child deal with the consequences. Hopefully it won't happen again.

6. How are the homework tasks recorded?

Is there a homework diary to fill in? Is the homework given verbally and needs to be written down? Is it copied from a board? Is your child expected to remember it?
Is that a problem if your child is slow at writing and copying? Would someone else do it for them? Sometimes schools have a texting system, which may help you be prepared if your child isn't sure what to do.

7. If your child doesn't know what to do, how would school suggest that could be managed?

I know of pupils who didn't know what to do, and neither parent nor child was clear how to handle this. No one knew how the school would expect this to be resolved. Ask. Perhaps a phone call to a friend is necessary. Get your child to do it. Otherwise write a note to the teacher to find out or get your child to ask the next day what it is. Remember, this is all part of the training to make your child independent and successful, depending on what you, your child and school have decided would be best.

8. If your child can't do it or doesn't understand it, what would school prefer you to do?

Resist the temptation to over-explain or take over the teaching. Remember the teacher will not know how much input you have had and may think your child can do it unaided and will move onto something more difficult. That would make it harder for them than handing in an unfinished piece of work full of mistakes.

Simply write a note to say how long was spent on it and why it is being returned incomplete. Teachers won't know unless you tell them. Your child may not feel comfortable explaining in front of everyone.

In my experience, children would prefer to take a dressing-down rather than admit they cannot do something or do not understand it - they feel silly and incompetent in front of their peers.

Help them by writing a note - it's much less demeaning or embarrassing and then the teacher can have a quiet word. If more parents did this, the teacher may soon get to see how the homework might need adjusting for more children.

9. Is your child expected to complete it on their own? Could they do it with a friend?

This is important. If it is your child's homework, IT'S NOT YOURS. If they can't do it, it is not your task to explain or teach them how to do it. If you do, the teacher will think your child is capable and give them something harder. Again, write a note to say your child tried but didn't understand whatever bit of it they told you. Then send it back. Any good teacher will then make sure your child has the relevant instruction to remedy this, and will come home with appropriate homework the next time.

On the other hand, doing it with a classmate would be beneficial to everyone. The one who understands it and can do it will explain it to the one who doesn't get it and it will reflect the way it has been taught in the classroom. Often, parents' help may be presented in a different way, which may be confusing: 'We don't do it like that.'

10. How much 'help' am I, as a parent, expected to give, if any?

I always ask parents this question -

me: 'Whose homework is it?'

parent: 'Well, it's my child's.'

me: 'So why are you 'helping' them do it then?'

parent: 'Well, they're struggling.'

me: 'Well, whose job is it to see that it is understood?'

parent: 'Well, the teacher I suppose.'

me: 'So if you 'help' your child, will the teacher realise that they are struggling?'

parent: 'Well, no I suppose not.'

me: 'So why do you do it?'

parent: 'Well, I don't want school to think I'm a useless parent, that I don't care, that I'll be seen as a failure for not helping my child, and they will fall behind and not get good SATs results and not get good exam results and won't get a good job - it's dog-eat-dog out there you know. . . . .'

This is why some parents 'help' their child.

On the other hand, many parents love to help, as do grandparents and carers. Another way of explaining things can sometimes be just what is needed, and teachers don't always have the time to cater for every child. It can depend on the homework too. An adult perspective can make learning together fun. It's also an opportunity to build relationships and perhaps create shared interests.

The answer is to find out if the homework is meant to be shared, or whether the teacher needs to know if the child can do it alone.

Find out what is expected from you from school and stick to it.

11. Ask for some guidance.

Ask if it would be possible for school to run classes for parents to show how children are taught these days. This is particularly true for Maths. Many parents try to show their children the way that they were taught, only to find that it leads to confusion, tears and upsets.

12. Does the school offer advice on how to motivate children to complete the homework, especially if it's met with resistance?

Find out what strategies the school uses and perhaps use the same ones. This supports the school and means you can work together.

13. Does it have to be presented in a certain way?

Find out what the homework is about and what the objective or the aim of it is. Does it always have to be written, for example? Perhaps your child could draw the answers, or tell you and you write it for them if writing is a challenge. Maybe do a cartoon strip, a poster, make a model or make a recording - you know how versatile children are these days - more 'techy' than most parents. It doesn't always have to be writing. This applies to secondary schools too, especially if your child is dyslexic or has different learning needs.

14. Has the homework been adapted for my child if they have special needs?

Make sure, especially if your child has a special need, that the homework is set at an appropriate level. There is nothing more disheartening than to get homework that is too easy or too hard. Both are a complete waste of time. Homework needs to be the right sort, at an appropriate level and for a specific reason.

15. When will it be marked?

Unless it is marked immediately, with specific feedback and discussion in order to improve learning and progress, there is no point doing the homework in the first place.

I have been told that often homework is not returned at all, or isn't marked until the end of term. Worse, children have spent ages doing it and it is never referred to again, or it has been handed in, put in a tray and forgotten about, never again to see the light of day. Not only is this a waste of everyone's time, it is demotivating for the child and an opportunity to improve and learn has been lost.

16. Who will mark it?

Find out who will mark it and when. Sometimes children mark each other's homework - it depends what sort of homework was given. Sometimes the teacher will mark it. Perhaps a classroom assistant will do it.

17. How will it be marked?

This is crucial, and I can't say it often enough.

Immediate, specific feedback leading to discussion in order to improve and progress is vital. It also needs to be consistent - the school may have a policy about it. Ask to see it. Otherwise, don't do the homework.

18. Would it be possible to set up a homework club in school?

I know of schools that have a homework 'club' during a lunchtime for children who haven't done their homework.

School sees it as an opportunity to complete it; the children see it as a punishment. There's obviously a miscommunication here that needs clarification.

Is there a time when children can get their homework done before they go home, preferably *not* a lunch time - that's a much needed break for children? Ask if staff could be there to supervise or help if needed. It doesn't have to be a silent thing - encourage the children to help each other. Everyone is a winner: the children get to have free time at home, teachers get feedback about their teaching and you have no hassle or tears or arguments about homework! Life at home will be less stressful and you will be proud to know that your children are becoming independent people, taking responsibility for their decisions.

(This is the way many private schools work. It's called 'prep', and is done straight after school and before tea and is supervised. The school day is longer, but at least the homework is out of the way, leaving evenings free for other things. Research shows this is one of the best methods for completing homework.)

Remember, peer to peer work is a very powerful way of learning, revising and improving.

19. Ask other parents to join you.

In Primary schools there is a 'mum's gate' group, who often stay and chat after they have seen their children safely into school, before they go off to work or whatever, and again when they are waiting to collect their children at the end of the school day. They discuss various things that are happening in school. Suppose you handed them this list of questions and set up a small group to discuss over a coffee or at work? If there is a consensus of opinion, perhaps ask your school to organise a bigger meeting, where homework is on the agenda and everyone could attend, rather than each parent asking individually. You don't have to do this on your own and it would benefit many people and their families, as well as teachers. Parameters would be clear and consistent.

Keep asking until everything is clear. That way, everyone knows where they stand and what needs to be done. Lack of information leads to confusion.

Chapter 8: The 'WHAM' Questions

In my experience, and from my research, parents expect homework, schools set it and children do it, but when I ask the following questions, I am met with blank looks, vague replies and different answers from all parties.

The previous chapter set out many questions in order to get you to think about homework in more detail. There are possibly too many to ask all in one go. I've condensed them into the 'WHAM' format. Asking the four main questions alone will lead to a conversation, and hopefully answer all the questions in each section.

Try putting the 'WHAM' questions to schools and teachers. (Print them off as a handy reminder. Feel free to adapt them to suit your own situation.) Do it every time your child moves to a new class and a new school. Homework policy may have changed in the holidays or be interpreted differently by some teachers, or may even be different for each subject area.

If the ground rules are clear for everyone, including the children, there are fewer arguments and upsets . . . guaranteed.

The 'WHAM' questions:

What is homework for . . . . .
> What sort of homework is it?
> What is it for?

How long should it take?
> Suppose my child forgets to bring it home or write it down?
> When should it be handed in?
> What happens if it's handed in late or not at all?
> Find out what happens if it's not completed or not done at all.
> Are there sanctions?

Am I expected to help?
> What if my child doesn't know what to do or doesn't understand it?
> If they can't or won't do it, what would you prefer me to do?
> Are they expected to do it on their own?
> How do you feel about children working together on it?
> How do you feel about me helping?
> What sort of help would you want \ expect me to give?
> Will you give me any guidance in the way you have taught my child so they will not get confused about teaching methods? e.g. maths

Marking
> What about marking - when will it be marked?
> How will it be marked: out of 10 or something else?
> Who will mark it?
> What sort of feedback will there be?

Chapter 9: Be prepared at home. Are you ready?

Make sure you have answers to all the questions in the previous chapter and your child is aware of them too. When everyone knows what is expected, it's much easier to get a good result.

Now it's time to set up the rules for home.

1. Discuss with your child the best time to do it.
Insisting on doing it immediately, to get it out of the way, is tough when they have just got back from school. They have worked hard all day (remember, they are only children) and need time to unwind and relax. You know how you feel after a day's work. Negotiate a good time for both of you and stick to it. Perhaps after a snack and before their favourite TV programme. Establishing a routine helps everyone's life flow more easily.

2. Make sure they have a space.
There may be a place you can set aside just for homework, complete with all the bits and pieces needed.
Turn off the TV, although some children say they work better with it on. Others may like some music in the background or to lie on the floor. Try it and see what works best.
Some parents let their child sit in the kitchen while they prepare tea. That way, you can keep an eye on progress and are on hand to offer encouragement and support. It also lets

them see that you too have work to do, and are not taking it easy and having fun while they beaver away.

3. Provide equipment.
Basics include pens, pencils, ruler, rubber, dictionary, thesaurus, paper, colouring pens or crayons. Other useful things could include scissors, sticky tape, Tippex, a calculator, stapler, hole punch, paper clips. Let your child loose in Poundland with some money and a list - good for Maths and budgeting - a life skill if ever there was one.
Keep everything all in one place so time is not lost searching for the right tools.
These days many homes have internet access for research. CDs and DVDs supplement this. Local libraries are great for resources and internet access as well as for reading books.
It's also a quiet place for secondary school pupils to go, away from home distractions if they need it.
As a bonus, libraries are free and a great way of spending a wet Saturday or holidays when you're stuck for something to keep them occupied.

4. Do not make a big fuss about it.
Explain that you both know how long it should take. You expect your child to do it themselves. When the time is up, you will add a note to the bottom of the work for the teacher, pointing out any tricky bits and how long it took, so they will have useful information to help them plan useful homework for the future.

You are on your child's side, but if they don't do the homework, or don't hand it in on time, they know what will happen and you will back the teacher up if there are repercussions.

No cajoling, threats or bribes allowed. If you have done the groundwork, everyone should be clear on how homework works.

Learning that one always has a choice and that there are consequences to one's decisions are very useful skills indeed. No point you or your child ranting, raving or crying about homework.

5. Make sure your child knows what to do, then let them get on with it.

You can provide a reassuring presence but try to let your child do it themselves. They know the parameters because you've previously discussed them.

6. Find a way of timing it.

When the time is up (you already know how long it should take) write a note on the bottom of the work saying this was what was achieved in the time and your child did it alone. If you helped in any way, add that in too. This is also useful for older children, who may sometimes get carried away and spend too long on it. In exam situations, time is of the essence, so sticking to homework times is good practice.

7. Praise effort and achievement

Focus on positive, specific praise. Being critical can shatter self-esteem, even if you think you're being helpful.

Be specific in your praise. If you say 'That's a good piece of work' your child won't have any idea what is good about it. Say something like 'Your handwriting is really neat and tidy, your teacher will be able to read that easily and you may get more marks for clear presentation.'

Or 'You checked your work very carefully and corrected the spellings all by yourself.'

Or 'You really stuck at that piece of homework, even though it seemed very tricky. You must be very proud of yourself that you finished it. That shows determination not to give up when something seems difficult.'

Specific detail lets them know exactly what they need to do to earn praise and experience success. Telling them exactly what is good means they will do it again.

8. Show an interest.

Even though it's not your homework, letting your child know that you are interested in it shows them that their life and what they do is important to you.

Taking them to libraries, providing DVDs or CDs to support them gives them a good start.

You may find you renew an interest in a forgotten topic, or learn something new and exciting yourself. It could even lead to visits or holidays for further investigation. One family I worked with took an annual holiday in Italy, based on what their son had been learning in school about the Romans. They had a wonderful time. It made a change from lying on the beach, wondering what to do next. This family was also inspired to take mini-breaks and days out to explore parts of the UK they had never been interested in before. You could use this as a reason to take a holiday in school time - it would be broadening your child's experience. Would school be able to provide the same experience? (Just saying!)

9. If your child gets upset or refuses point blank to do it.

Have a chat to find out why there is such resistance. Who knows what goes on in children's minds! If you have done the groundwork, this should not arise, but if it does, do not panic. Try to ascertain what the problem is, but if all else fails, offer to write a note to the teacher explaining that your child was too distressed to do the homework, you were unable to get to the bottom of it and let the teacher deal with it the next day.

10. Resist the urge to correct it yourself.

This is the teacher's job. Maybe ask your child to check it themselves, but the teacher needs to know where mistakes have been made. Mistakes equal feedback and a learning opportunity. No mistakes means the teacher thinks it can be done easily and may give something harder next time, leading to more pressure on you and your child. Everyone learns from their mistakes, but the *teacher* needs to know what those mistakes were. You are not really helping your child by correcting their work.

11. Set up a homework club with one or two of your child's friends.

This relieves the pressure on you and means your child will be more interested in doing it.

If one child doesn't understand, then the other(s) can explain. This is a sound strategy that benefits everyone - explaining something so that others understand means that the person doing the explaining really knows it too. Reward with a celebration tea and maybe a favourite TV programme or time on a video game. Carrot, no stick. Works every time!

(This worked really well with one of my students. Weekends were a battlefield and everyone was fed up with homework. Then I suggested this: ask a friend over so it could be done together, and they could help each other. This family went a step further. The two sisters invited a friend each, their mum set them up with tables etc, timed the homework and then they all had pizza and a fun afternoon on the trampoline. Everyone happy. Not only that, the next time the girls themselves got everything ready.)

(When I was doing my degree, aged 43, we used to meet up for revision sessions in Roger's house and test each other. Many brains find the gaps. Mini chocolate rolls helped a lot too.)

Remember, peer to peer work is a very powerful way of learning, revising and improving.

Chapter 10: Do it differently

This strategy involves the school in a big way, and offers a new look at what homework could be. You may believe it to be a fantasy, but dreams can come true.

Homework doesn't have to be limited to what it is already. Remember, each school decides for itself what the homework policy will be.

Suppose it was possible to do something different, which satisfied the school's criteria yet made homework _fun,_ especially in Primary schools?

Suppose homework tasks were set in a completely different way?

Cast your mind back to the introduction when I told you about the square tomatoes and egg in a bottle.
Back then I was astounded how much enthusiasm was created, and how many children were inspired to race home to find the solutions by the next day. They craved to find out, were eager to put the time in to achieve it, and engaged everyone in it.
My egg and tomato challenge was thrown out on the spur of the moment because I could see the children were transfixed and left in suspense because I didn't tell them how I'd done it. The urge to solve a mystery was enough to send them off to try it themselves.

That's the response I think homework should create, if it's to be done at all.

What if that excitement could be replicated with current homework but without the fear of repercussions if it weren't completed?

Suppose the children had some say in the matter and could choose to do it or not, without fear of staying in if they didn't choose to do it?

What if they could SUGGEST IDEAS OF THEIR OWN that everyone else, including the teachers, could join in with?

Suppose it meant they didn't need reminding to do it and it kept them happily occupied without you standing over them or nagging them to get it done?

What if you got excited about it as well instead of it being a chore?

Suppose you could suggest things too?

Brainstorm this idea with other parents, your children and their friends. Does it get them excited too?

What if this group of parents then approached the Head Teacher and said something like this:

"We realise that homework is a part of school life now, at every stage of our children's education. We also realise that we all need to work together in the best interests of our children, your targets and expectations. We also need you to know that homework in its present form creates difficulties at home. There are time constraints - our children have busy lives outside of school. We are working parents and have limited time to spend making sure that homework is

completed. It can be a battleground, and we can all get frustrated, upset and rebellious, especially when it's Sunday night and the homework is still sitting there.
What if we could do it differently?
Suppose we worked together so that homework reflected the 'end' instead of 'the means to the end'?
Would you be open to suggestions to try a different format for a term and see if it works?
How would it be if we encouraged the children to set the homework instead?"

Then present something like this, or whatever you can come up with.

Free up the concept of homework: you don't have to do it. This immediately takes away the pressure on free time, and releases teachers from marking it.

Suggest there could be a homework afternoon, perhaps a Friday or a Monday. In the beginning it could take the form of a 'show and tell' afternoon, encouraging children to be confident in presenting their ideas to others. It may develop in other ways once everyone gets used to it. Set parameters e.g. nothing silly or dangerous, and maybe a time limit.
Choose a theme for the week. It could be related to school work or maybe one of those objectives homework is supposed to achieve. Ask the children \ students to come up with ideas and put them in a hat. Pull one idea out each week. Everyone, including the teacher, is encouraged to do it, but there are no

sanctions if you don't. No judgement. No excuses needed. Just "I didn't choose to do this." No restrictions on how it is presented. It could be written, drawn, painted, modelled, sung, danced, powerpoint, photo-ed, You tubed . . .

When the homework afternoon arrives, treat it with respect. Make sure it happens and is not overridden by other things. Give it the same status as Maths or English. There may not be right or wrong answers to this homework. It may depend on the task. How exciting it would be to see what comes up, and how many ways it would be interpreted and presented.

Children don't have to do it on their own either - no restrictions on a group activity or two or three people working together (teamwork and communication - important skills in the workplace).

Some ideas may need to be started one week but need longer to come to fruition. In the meantime, you can do a few more. (This encourages multi-tasking, stamina, and determination. You may be surprised that the children you thought might stay with a task may not be the ones that do it.)

Here are a few suggestions to get you going. These ideas are probably more suited to primary schools because that is where I spent most of my time. Secondary school may require a more subject-based approach, but nonetheless it could still be creative and fun.

I'm sure you can think of many more.

Remember - make it as much fun as you can. Then you'll find that no-one wants to be left out.

Some of these things may already be done at school, but not in the context of homework.

The idea is to give children some choice, to let them use their imagination to inspire others. I'm not sure how much input children have at the moment, and they are an untapped resource.

Just be aware of the skills involved in what you are asking them to do. If there's a purpose for something, and it's fun, people learn without realising it. They are using what they have learned to solve a problem.

I'm aware that some of those are completely random, and might not be appropriate at all. I'm just playing around with the idea of doing it differently, that's all. It's just to get you thinking about homework, what it is for, how else it could be presented and to ask schools to view it from a different angle.

You may like homework as it is. On the other hand, this might strike a chord with you and tempt you into making choices about what it is and how you do it.

It's up to you.

Primary School Ideas:

1. Grow a vegetable, look after it, bring it to school and we'll cook it.
2. Make a cake to share. Sell it to make funds for school or a charity.
3. Your favourite possession: bring it in, talk about it, draw it. Say why it is your favourite. (One child brought his grandpa.)
4. Do a good deed without being asked. Report back to say how it was received, or even if anyone noticed.
5. Surprise your teacher \ class with something related to the work in school during the last week. It might not even relate to your own class, but could be something that caught your interest elsewhere.
6. Say what you find easy. (not necessarily school work; it could be tying shoe laces or knowing when someone is upset)
7. Say what you find hard. (again, not necessarily school work)
8. One thing you are good at
9. One thing you're not so good at.
10. One quality you've noticed about your best friend that makes them shine.
11. Read something you've never read before.
12. Read something your friend recommends.
13. Do something you've never tried before.
14. Eat something you've never tried before. Bring some in for others to try.
15. Go somewhere you've never been before.
16. Tell your parents about your favourite place and why.

17. Interview a family member about something.
18. Listen to a piece of music and dance to it.
19. Go for a walk along the canal \ the road \ in the forest. Look for something you haven't noticed before. Take a photo of it, draw it or paint it.
20. Make a model of something. Anything.
21. Make a list of 10 things you'd like to do before you leave school.
22. 10 things you'd like to do after you leave school.
23. 10 things about . . . . . .
24. Dress up as someone.
25. Find out 5 things about . . . .
26. 5 things you are grateful for.
27. Try a new form of exercise or a new sport.
28. Make a collection of something.
29. Tidy your room without being asked and see if anyone notices and what is said.

There you go - 29 weeks' worth, and I wasn't even trying.

As for Secondary Schools, I have a few ideas . . .

1. Go on to a fuel comparison site and see how much money you could save on your fuel bills. Parents have no time to do this and students find it an enjoyable challenge, not a chore. There might even be a reward \ commission to be negotiated here. Can you convert the units of gas used into kw\hour, using the formula on the back of the gas bill?

2. Help your parents decide on a menu for the week, cost it out and save them some money. Use online shopping baskets and get it delivered. Use the time and money saved for a family treat or put in a holiday fund which pays interest.

3. Start a savings account. Research the interest rates. I had pocket money from an early age and had to save half and spend half. By the time I was 17 I had saved enough money to buy a second-hand car.

4. Learn to cook a meal for the family. One student went to University knowing how to cook chilli for 5 people. He ate one lot, froze some and sold the rest to students who couldn't cook. There are lots of students who can't cook because they've been too busy studying to pass exams to get to University.

5. Volunteer to walk someone's dog. Take a friend.

6. Chat to an old person. Ask them what school was like for them, or what they were good at.

7. List 10 things you are grateful for.

8. Spend time daydreaming every day, building your future in your mind.

9. Find out how many organisations there are where you live that cater for young people like you. Would you join one, or help out?

10. Write a letter (not an email or a text) to someone thanking them for something they have done for you. Do not underestimate the effect this will have - they will be thrilled, because it is something they can keep and refer to whenever they may feel a bit down. It will cheer them up. Notice how it makes you feel too.

11. Read the labels on an item in the supermarket. Research all the words you are not familiar with and decide if you would still buy the product when you know what the ingredients are.

12. Grow something edible and compare the taste to the same item from a shop.

13. Learn to use a drill, a saw, a hammer.

14. Learn to play an instrument.

15. Listen to music that is different from your usual sort.

16. Find out what happens to all the water you use every day.

17. Learn how to change a plug.

18. Learn how to meditate.

19. Walk round the streets where you live and pay attention to how much litter has been dropped.

20. Can you name all the shops near you in the right order?

21. Learn First Aid. (why isn't this a core subject from the word go?)

22. After ¾ hour studying, take a brisk walk for 15 mins and see how much better you feel and what difference it makes to your work afterwards. Suggest your parents go with you.

They'll thank you for it when they find their blood pressure improves and their weight decreases.
23. Learn to juggle.
24. Wash the family car for love.
25. Find out *exactly* what your parents do all day while you are at school.
26. Try to teach your parents what you learned in one of your classes today (guaranteed they will find it hard).
27. Learn how to clean the bathroom. (you'll have to do it some day)
28. Find out 5 things about the European Community.
29. List 5 things you'd like to give back to the world.
30. List 10 things you'd like to experience before you 'settle down.' Compare notes with your friends and family.
31. Read a copy of the 'Big Issue.'
32. Try doing without electricity, your phone, computer, ipad etc for a day and night. What happened to your head? How did you manage it?
33. Start researching your Family History. Ask questions of your oldest family member before it's too late.
34. Re-decorate your room. Yourself. It's a useful life skill.

Chapter 11: Opt out

What if you have read all the pros and cons, tried all the strategies that have already been suggested and you are still unhappy about homework?

Would you consider opting out of it altogether? It isn't as controversial as you may think and all over the world there are places where homework is disappearing.

I'm not advocating marching into school one day and demanding your child has no more homework at all, ever. It would be a decision taken after exploring all the options and talking about it to a lot of people over a period of time, because I don't for one minute think that homework will disappear overnight from every school in the land. Change happens slowly, often far too slowly for my liking, but it can be encouraged if supported by well-researched information and presented in a calm, co-operative manner. (Those of you who know me well will know that my preferred style is 'just do it', but when dealing with a huge public organisation that never happens.)

I was reading Richard Templar's 'The Rules of Parenting' the other day. He set out a useful distinction between home and school:
'Although your child will spend more hours in school than with you during term time, they need to feel you are interested, concerned and involved, albeit at a distance.'

He said "Schools give you information. Being 'schooled' is not the same thing as being 'educated'. Teachers are there to pass on information and coach them towards doing well for their exams. Exams are how teachers, schools and children are measured.

"You, as parents, on the other hand, are not your child's teacher. You can allow them to be wrong and learn for themselves without correcting them. You can emphasise all the life skills that school isn't there for and which cannot be measured. Those things are maybe more important than academic achievement. You can encourage your children to try new things, discover new interests, meet new people. You can encourage them to read more widely, take an interest in the world, ask questions and form their own opinions.

"Schools can easily dominate your child's life at times and that's when you are needed to keep it in perspective. You don't want school to permeate every part of their lives."

I think this is where homework has become troublesome for many people. It oversteps the line between being helpful and manageable and becomes stressful and counter-productive.

It needs reining in a bit, or even dispensing with altogether, especially as children are given homework as soon as they start school. In some cases, children are only just 4 years old. They may even have been given things to do at home when they were in Nursery or pre-school. This country manages to instil the habit of taking work home from a very young age.

Richard Templar suggests letting up on the pressure.

"In the end it has to be their choice how hard they work. Everyone keeps telling them they need to get good grades, to pass exams, and their whole life may depend on this. Well, the chances are, it doesn't.
"Think about how much stress your child has about the exam thing. Do you really need to add to that? There are more important things in life than academic achievement and people who fail exams do go on to become happy, fulfilled adults. Doing well in exams is wonderful but it's not the end of the world if they don't."

He adds " The way to highlight the implications isn't to tell them to work harder, watch less TV or stop going out with their friends, but to ask questions such as 'How do you rate your chances of passing? Have you thought about what will happen if you don't pass?'
Home is the one place they can escape from all the pressure - it's your job to help them learn self-discipline by NOT making them work."

Following on from that there are other things to consider about homework.

Alfie Kohn, the USA's most outspoken critic of education's fixation on grades and test scores, was interviewed by 'Family Circle' in 2012. He said homework drives kids away from learning. He says:

'Let kids be kids and provide them with time to grow socially, physically, emotionally and artistically.'

He asks these questions about homework:

1. Research fails to find any academic benefit for students younger than 15. Do you have reason to believe they should be given work anyway?
2. Should children be required to devote their afternoons and evenings to academic tasks (at the expense of social, artistic, physical development) or is 5 or 6 hours a day sufficient?
3. In your opinion, who should determine what happens during family time - families or schools?
4. If all students in a class (considering their different backgrounds, interests aptitudes) have the same homework, how likely is it that will lead to optimal learning?
5. Does homework seem designed to deepen understanding of important ideas? Does it have that effect?
6. Is the effect on children's desire to learn positive or negative as a result of homework? Should homework be on a regular basis or when it's needed?
7. Should it be voluntary? Or those who want it can have it? What about other activities? Are you as a parent afraid that your child will be outstripped by others?

A Stanford researcher in the USA, Denise Pope, found that too much homework has negative effects on student well-being and behavioural engagement. (10th March 2014).

Amanda Enayati, CNN contributor asks "Is homework making your child sick?" (21st March 2014)
Cheltenham Ladies' College is considering a homework ban over student welfare. This is one of Britain's most prestigious schools, and homework could be abolished in order to tackle an 'epidemic' of teenage depression and anxiety. (6th June 2015)

Professor Dylan Wiliam thinks homework is a waste of time unless it is completed in guided hours, and cites the private school way of doing homework as being the best way. He thinks revision of work done in class with a test the next day is a good thing. Effective marking and feedback is crucial because constructive comments and discussion cause thinking, show you how to do it and improve.

The French President, Francois Hollande, says work should be done at school rather than at home, at the end of the school day, on school premises. He has banned homework in primary schools.

A Cape Town school in South Africa is leading the way in the education sector by doing away with homework; six months later they're seeing surprising results. (Nov 23 2015)

Go back to 'Chapter 5: No it isn't' and refresh your memory about why homework is not a good idea.

That's the picture given by experts, research and the media in several countries other than the UK and there are more links at the end of the book. Google 'homework' and see what you can find. Every year something new pops up, with more research worldwide gaining momentum, both for and against.

It makes you think, as here in the UK we give homework to children as young as 4, training them that it is expected and acceptable to bring work home. Keep in mind how <u>you</u> feel when you get home after work and the last thing you want to do is more of what you've just left behind.

Could you imagine a life where the conversation wasn't 'Have you done your homework?' but 'Tell me what's interested you most this week? What's inspired you or annoyed you? What would you like to change? What would you like to contribute to this world?'

Think about how the time spent on homework now could be used differently if there were no homework, bearing in mind the following research from UNICEF:
"In 2007 a UNICEF survey of childhood asked: 'Do you find your classmates kind and helpful?' Fewer than 50% of UK children said yes.
Recent studies concluded that is down to our unquestioning acceptance of the ethics of hyper-competitive consumerism.

In 2009 the 'Good Childhood Report' stated that a key reason for children's social and emotional problems was a national culture of selfish individualism.

In 2011, a follow-up report on the UNICEF survey stated loud and clear that infant lack of well-being is rooted in our materialistic culture. It found that, while parents believed their children needed lots of fashionable gadgets and other consumer goods, **their children said they'd prefer more family time and the opportunity to play out."**

Opting out of homework would free up time for those things.

Take some time to really think about homework. Talk about it with your friends, your children, your school. You don't have to do anything revolutionary; just mention it in passing over a coffee. Just raising the subject is a start. Use the information in this book to start a discussion. Up until now, homework has been accepted as the norm. Lots of people moan about it interfering with home life but still do it. No one admits that it is a struggle, for fear of being cast as a bad parent or failing their child. No one seems to have the courage to stand up and say 'Enough!' Remember, homework is not compulsory.

Talking with other parents might reveal others who think as you do. Putting a case together that includes facts and figures and research might open a discussion with teachers, the Head and Governors around homework in general, especially if you have tried the 'WHAM' approach and already have a great working relationship with the school. It might even persuade the Head to survey the whole school to find out the strength of opinion, or even try 'no homework' for a trial period to see what happens.

You could discuss other options with your child, You'd have to make sure that one form of constraint would not be replaced by another. The time spent in other pursuits would need to be joyful, co-operative and in everyone's best interests. You might even consider some of the ideas in Chapter 10.

I don't for one minute think that all schools will immediately drop homework, these things take time, but sowing the seeds will bring it out into the open and make for a more transparent approach to it. That's all I'm hoping for - planting a seed or two, to see what will flourish.

In all cases where schools have opted out of homework, the results were positive and not one school regretted it. Tests and exam results have not worsened and in some cases they have been bettered. There are indications that children are reading more, which can only be a good thing. Removing the stress, upsets and time constraints has been beneficial.

Some parents insist on homework. Perhaps some parents might insist it stops.

Give it a try - take it out and see what life is like without homework.

Chapter 12: Have you changed your mind?

This book set out to give you strategies to manage your children's homework and also to challenge your opinion of homework, to make you think what it is all for and what to do about it.

I hope it has succeeded, even if it has only made you think about it a little bit, and I hope you have found something in this book that you didn't know before. You may not agree with what I have written but perhaps I have raised issues that others secretly believe and are reluctant to admit to.

Some people love homework and think it can improve the chances of doing well in the world, as well as developing a child in many ways. On the other hand, many parents are uneasy about homework. Many teachers find it a trial to set and mark homework when they would rather be planning exciting lessons. Many children and students are overwhelmed by homework.

Even though there are mutterings, it seems as if homework is accepted as an integral part of school life. Even though I have worked with students and families who are distressed by homework, they will still do the work, because otherwise there are fears of not being a good parent, their child will fall behind or miss out, or they still don't realise homework is not compulsory. It is difficult to make a stand on their own to change the face of homework in their schools.

The question to ask is 'what is best for <u>your</u> child?' Does homework fit with their values, dreams and aspirations, which may not necessarily be the same as yours? How will you as a family position yourselves around homework? Are you for it or against? Will you decide to stay with it, change it or opt out altogether?

Which camp were you in and have you changed your mind?

Books, articles and links references

The homework myth - why our kids get too much of a bad thing. Alfie Kohn. 2007

The Rules of Parenting. Richard Templar.

21st century girls - how the modern world is damaging our daughters and what we can do about it. Sue Palmer. Orion Books. 2014

HT: the homework debate: All work and no play? Judith Judd. TES newspaper
19 June 2009
www.tes.co.uk/article.aspx?storycode=6015783

Is it time to scrap homework? Irena Barker. TES magazine. 15 February 2013
www.tes.co.uk/article.aspx?storycode=6319948

Bringing down barriers in KS3. NUT. 16 November 2009
http://www.teachers.org.uk/node/1050

The 4 most common types of homework MacBeath and Turner 1990
http://www.theguardian.com/education/2004/feb/09/schools.uk

The burden of homework is too heavy. Peter Stanford. The Independent 9 October 2008
http://www.independent.co.uk/news/education/schools/peter-stanford-the-burden-of-homework-is-too-heavy-955005.html

Effect of homework on school gains. Hazel Denver et al. November 1999
http://www.bsrlm.org.uk/IPs/ip19-3/BSRLM-IP-19-3-10.pdf

A life in secondary teaching - finding time for learning. Cambridge University.
NFER research
https://www.educ.cam.ac.uk/people/staff/galton/aLiSTreport.pdf

Who benefits from homework assignments? Marte Ronning.
Marte Rønning - SSB
www.ssb.no/publikasjoner/DP/pdf/dp566.pdf

Money's too tight to mention. NUT. The Teacher. January\February 2015
http://www.teachers.org.uk/magazine/january-february-2015/text/a18.html

Ask the question: triple marking. NUT. The Teacher. January\February 2015
http://www.teachers.org.uk/magazine/january-february-2015/text/a34.html

Long homework hours for families. Sean Coughlan. BBC News, Education and Family.
www.bbc.com/news/education-30417132

End homework. ATL. 2008
www.parentsoutloud.com/end-homework/hashsthash.gtA7uhMf.dpuf

Two hours' homework a night linked to better school results. The Guardian. Department of Education. 29 March 2012
www.theguardian.com/education/2012/mar/29/homework-linked-better-school-results

Is homework making your child sick? Amanda Enayati. Manchester Evening News.
12 May 2015
www.cnn.com/2014/03/21/health/homework-stress

Exam stress: children as young as 10 worry SATs results will affect their future - and their schools' league table place. Charlotte Dobson. Manchester Evening news. 12 May 2015
www.manchestereveningnews.co.uk/news/greater-manchester-news/sats-test-children-stress-exams-9240803

New term, new battle over homework. Katherine Sellgren. 24 September 2014
www.bbc.co.uk/news/education-24126000

Stanford research shows pitfalls of homework. Clifton B Parker. Stanford Evening News. 10 March 2014
www.news.stanford.edu/news/2014/march/too-much-homework-031014

The case against homework. Alfie Kohn. Family Circle.com. October 2012
www.alfiekohn.org

Cheltenham Ladies' College considers homework ban over student welfare. The Guardian, The Times, The Daily Mail. 6 June 2015
www.theguardian.com/education/2015/jun/06/cheltenham-ladies-college-considers-homework-ban-over-student-welfare

CAPE TOWN SCHOOL DITCHES HOMEWORK
November 23, 2015 by Jonathan Meyer
www.capetownetc.com/blog/news/cape-town-school-ditches-homework
 http://www.capetownetc.com/blog/news/cape-town-school-ditches-homework/#sthash.Ac7hNpt1.dpuf)

Before you go . .

I see you have made it all the way to the end of my book. I'm glad you enjoyed it enough to finish it. I'm a self-published writer and it would be a tremendous help if you would take a minute out of your busy schedule to leave a review for me on the sales page on Amazon. Your review will let readers know what to expect and what you liked about this book.
I'm looking forward to reading your review
Thank you so much for your feedback.

Jan Evans

Printed in Great Britain
by Amazon